The Alcázar of Seville: The History of Spain's Most Famous Royal Palace

By Charles River Editors

Guy Moll's picture of the Patio de la Montería courtyard

About Charles River Editors

Charles River Editors is a boutique digital publishing company, specializing in bringing history back to life with educational and engaging books on a wide range of topics. Keep up to date with our new and free offerings with this 5 second sign up on our weekly mailing list, and visit Our Kindle Author Page to see other recently published Kindle titles.

We make these books for you and always want to know our readers' opinions, so we encourage you to leave reviews and look forward to publishing new and exciting titles each week.

Introduction

Jose Luis Filpo Cabana's picture of the Patio del Yeso portico

The majority of those fortunate enough to feast their eyes upon the majestic complex that is the Alcázar of Seville share the same sentiment: its beauty is indescribable. This is a place that oozes opulence, a kind of opulence flavored by class and historical charm, rather than the garish flamboyance and tawdry ostentation often displayed by the nouveau riche. To say that the Alcázar is fit for the fussiest prince would simply be downplaying its splendor. Of course, this was exactly what the Alcázar was, and continues to be, for this fantastical compound is the oldest European royal residence still in use.

The royal estate, with 17,000 square meters of spectacular structures and 7 hectares of lavish gardens, is even more sublime in the nighttime. The rambling Moorish arches, and the gorgeous detail of the fairy-tale turrets and curtain walls – from the striking shapes of the rectangular merlons, capped with triangular cones, to the coarse, aged texture and smears of damp discoloring the ancient facade – are all the more emphasized by the torches dotted throughout the premises. But following the departure of the nocturnal visitors, the interactive tour guides (clad in elaborate costumes of historical figures just hours before), and the last of the staff, the Alcázar, some say, becomes an intoxicating, sinister maze almost impossible to escape.

The Alcázar of Seville: The History of Spain's Most Famous Royal Palace journeys through the eventful timeline of the palatial fortress, as well as the stages leading up to its fruition. It also explores some of the fascinating characters who lived there, and the most pivotal events that took place within the centuries-old brick walls. Along with pictures of important people, places, and events, you will learn about the Alcázar of Seville like never before.

Prologue

Even if one were to discount security and the Spanish royals who reside here seasonally, legend has it that the Alcázar is never truly uninhabited. Take a post-midnight stroll through the colonnades or the baths, and listen closely, insist mystics, and one will hear the spine-tingling sniffling, harrowing whimpers, and wretched weeping of the hapless souls who met their demise at the hands of Pedro the Cruel, Peter I of Castile, one of the many builders and tenants of this bewitching place. The vicious and volatile wrath of the cruel monarch knew no bounds, and his victims, no numbers. Some say these cries belong to the young maidens who were burnt at the stake for no other reason than rejecting Pedro's romantic advances. Others say they come from the spirit of Eleanor of Guzman, the mistress of Pedro's father, Alfonso XI of Castile, and one of Pedro's first kills. Or perhaps they come from all of Pedro's victims, cursed by their violent deaths to roam the Alcázar in perpetuity.

Luis Garcia's picture of a 16th century statue of Pedro the Cruel

A depiction of Alfonso XI of Castile in Froissart's chronicles

Like Alfonso, Pedro smote anyone who opposed, threatened, or displeased him in any way, no matter how trivial. Eleanor, however, was one Pedro executed out of sheer vengeance. When Alfonso was still in power, the philandering sovereign unabashedly neglected his wife, Maria of Portugal, along with their children, Fernando and Pedro, treasuring instead his relationship with Eleanor, and the 10 children she bore him. Eleanor was revered by state officials and nobility by default, and acted as Alfonso's de facto consort, dipping her toes and pitching in her 2 cents to all matters of the state. 8-year-old Fadrique Alfonso, among the brood of 10, was appointed Grand Master of the Order of Santiago, a Christian order of Spanish knights that aimed to vanquish Spanish Saracens and guard the pilgrims that trekked to the shrine of the *Santiago de Compostela* (more on him later).

Shortly after Alfonso's death in late March of 1350, courtesy of the plague, 16-year-old Pedro, working in tandem with the embittered dowager, accused Eleanor of stirring up a revolt, confined her to the dungeons, and had her executed in the city of Talavera de la Reina a year later. Apart from the multiple assertions of Eleanor's innocence falling on deaf ears, the helpless captive was subjected to a slow and hideous death. Some say her executioners crudely sliced her neck open with a butcher's cleaver. Others say she was left tethered to a post with the cord pinching her neck, left to starve under the unforgiving sun until she eventually perished from exposure days later.

Even Pedro's chief advisers and the formerly untouchable aristocracy were apparently reduced to quaking sycophants and bootlickers in his presence, for they, too, were expendable in the king's eyes. Their nerves became further strained when Gutier Fernández de Toledo, who remained an integral part of Pedro's cortége for over a decade as a decorated military commander, diplomat, and court official, was unwittingly thrust upon the chopping block in 1360. Gutier, who Pedro suspected was fraternizing with the enemy, was ambushed by assassins disguised as negotiators, and beheaded. Before the doomed man was killed, he was allowed to pen one final – and many say prophetic – letter to Pedro: "My Lord...I kiss your hands and take leave of you, now to journey before an even greater lord than yourself...At the moment of my death, I give you my final counsel – if you do not put aside the dagger, if you do not stop committing such murders, then you shall lose your realm and place your person in the greatest jeopardy..."

Pedro took no heed of Gutier's wise words and ordered the deaths of foes and friends alike with the kind of casual indifference one maintains when ordering lunch. Likewise, this extended to Pedro's callous and disrespectful treatment of his victims' bodies. Castilian noble Garcilaso de la Vega II was another who inadvertently wandered into his execution in 1351. His headless body was then tossed out of the Alcázar's tallest tower and into the street, where it was trampled upon by a stampede of bulls. Infante Juan of Aragón, who like the others was deceived into parting with his weapons, met a similar fate. The prince's cold corpse was also tossed out of the window, and the remnants later dumped in the River Guadalquivir.

Such morbidly riveting tales only scratch the surface when it comes to the colorful tapestry of history that has unfolded, and continues to unfold, in the Alcázar. In the same breath, Pedro is only one of the fascinating characters who inhabited these fabled grounds, which many deem the most dazzling "jewel in Seville's crown." But this paradisaical complex of enchanting palaces and gardens is far more than just an impressive landmark – it is evidence of the beauty birthed from the multicultural Andalusian timeline, a harmonious masterpiece crafted by Muslims, Christians, and Jews.

A Ruby Arising from Blood

"...I hear voices crying, 'Yield! That is true wisdom!'

But I reply, 'Poison would be a sweeter draught to me

Than such a cup of shame!'

...the barbarians wrest me from my realm,

And my soldiers forsake me...

When I fell upon the foe...

Hoping for death, I flung myself into the fray;

But alas, my hour had not yet come!" - Mutamid Ibn Abbad, the Poet-King of Seville, upon losing the Alcázar

In order to fully appreciate the wonder that is the Alcázar, it's necessary to understand the history of Seville and the events leading up to its creation.

Seville has most likely been occupied since the Neolithic Era by enterprising people who wished to capitalize on the fertile land and the Guadalquivir, the second-longest river in all of Spain. In the 1st century BCE, Seville, a river port and bridge between Andalusia and the Atlantic, was transformed into a bustling commercial crossroads between the North-East and Western Iberian territories by the Romans. The Roman settlers proceeded to rule the land now known as Seville for more than 600 years.

The first Roman colony in the area, which was christened "Italica" by its founders, lay about 6 miles from modern-day Seville. Under its competent conquerors, Italica swiftly evolved into a vibrant metropolis serviced by aqueducts, a 25,000-seater amphitheater, and iconic Romanesque structures. It was in this luxurious locale that the future Roman emperors Trajan and Hadrian were born.

An ancient bust of Trajan

A bust of Hadrian in Venice

In 49 BCE, Italica was renamed "Hispalis" by Julius Caesar, and it continued to expand under Caeasar and his successors, in time encompassing a significant portion of what is now Seville today.

The plot that would one day become the Alcázar, situated close to the literal heart of Seville, was turned into the grounds of the Collegium, or College of Olearians, in the 1st century CE. *Collegia*, as defined by William Smith in *The Dictionary of Greek & Roman Antiquities,* were "civic, religious, or fraternal associations." Whether the Collegium of Olearians served specifically as a guild for businessmen, a burial society, or a social club, is uncertain; one can only assume that the association was equipped with a governing body modeled after the Senate of Rome, and that the club boasted a *curia*, or a meeting hall.

Not much, if anything, is known about the Roman establishment's appearance, but excavations conducted in recent years have given archaeologists a glimpse of its décor, as well as the construction materials the Romans might have utilized. The green hues found on 30 fragments of Romanesque wall paintings lifted from the excavation site of the Patio de Banderas, for instance, is believed to be a mix of celadonite and chlorite. "Refractive materials," such as crushed glass, and light-refracting minerals were used to create shades of Egyptian-blue.

In the early years of the 5th century CE, Seville was seized by a Central European tribe known as the "Silingi Vandals" from Silesia, but their dominion over Seville was short-lived, for they were quickly ousted and replaced by the nomadic Germanic tribespeople otherwise known as the Visigoths in the year 461 CE. The Visigoths swept away the ruins of the *collegium*, not wanting this valuable plot of land to go to waste, and in its stead, erected a basilica dedicated to deacon-turned-saint Vincent of Saragossa, a native of Huesca and the first martyr of Spain. There appears to be no surviving sketches or descriptions of this particular church, but it is safe to assume that it shared many of the characteristics of other Visigothic churches in Spain at the time.

It would be reasonable to assume that like Spain's oldest church, raised by Visigothic King Recceswinth in the 7th century CE in honor of San Juan de Banos, the St. Vincent Basilica in Seville was fashioned out of dry ashlar stone blocks, and consisted of 3 aisles, "latticed windows" chiseled out of stone, and walls frescoed with decorative, rather than religiously symbolic imagery. The basilica's arches would have most likely been somewhat shaped like a horseshoe, a distinctive architectural feature that were supposedly the creation of either the Visigoths or 3rd century Syrians. These so-called "horseshoe arches" became associated with Muslims in Iberia later on, for it was the Moors who popularized the design and incorporated it into many of their structures. Visitors with a trained eye can still spot the Visigothic shafts and capitals still used in the Palace of Peter of Castile (Pedro the Cruel) today.

It was reportedly in the St. Vincent Basilica that the Visigoths buried Saint Isidore of Seville, who was, as the Spanish council of bishops who canonized him in 653 called him, "an illustrious teacher of our time and the glory of the Catholic Church." This pious figure also authored the *Etymologiae*, the first comprehensive encyclopedia written from a Catholic point of view. Here, Isidore's sacred body lay in a handsome stone tomb until the basilica was dismantled, after which his body was then relocated to a church in Leon. The tombstone of Honorato, Bishop of Seville, may have also been housed in the St. Vincent Basilica for some time, but it was later transferred to the Seville Cathedral.

Seville slipped into the hands of the Moors in the year 712, and chroniclers attribute this consequential turn of events to the insatiable sexual appetite of Rodrigo, the last king of the Spanish Visigoths. In 711, Rodrigo kidnapped, raped, and fell in love with a young woman by the name of Florinda, who was taking a dip in the Rio Tajo when he chanced upon her. The highly abusive and toxic qualities to their "relationship" aside, Florinda, as it turns out, was none other than the youngest daughter of Rodrigo's comrade, Count Julian. Outraged by Rodrigo's betrayal, Julian partnered with the Moorish Emir Muda bin Nusayr and concocted a plan to take Spain for themselves. In the autumn of 711, General Tariq ibn Ziyan and a fleet of war vessels containing an army of 9,000 strong ventured out from the North African coast and forged across the azure waters of the Gibraltar Strait. Weeks later, the Moorish soldiers reached the coast of southern Spain and descended upon the foreign land. The Moors, evidently, were here to stay, and their raids eventually reached as far as the Pyrenees. For the next 5 centuries, the Moors presided over a substantial amount of Spanish terrain, their customs and art inevitably bleeding into the local culture.

Emir Muda bin Nusayr was resolved to make his intentions of permanent residency known to his new subjects. For starters, the metropolis of Hispalis was rebranded "Ixbilia," and the Betis River renamed the "Guad el Kevir." The names "Ixbilia" and "Guad el Kevir" became so tightly tied to the locals' identity that future generations opted to retain the Moorish roots of both names. Not long after, the emir ordered the destruction of St. Vincent's Basilica in Seville. Massive squares of vegetation, gravel, and fauna surrounding the defunct basilica were also cleared to make room for the new fortress and palace that would be constructed in its place. The Moors named this new complex the "Real Alcázar (Royal Alcázar)," derived from the Arabic word "*al-qasr,*" meaning "fortress," and its synonym, "*castillo,*" meaning "castle." The Alcázar, as demanded by the emir, was to be mighty enough to withstand all attacks from Vikings, vengeful Visigoths, and other potential enemies.

In the year 913, the Caliph of Cordoba, Abdurrahman III an-Nasir, commissioned the construction of a network of new government buildings. The Dar al-lmara, as the caliph called it, was to be built in the south of the city, furnished with defensive walls that encircled the Old Town of Seville, including the original Alcázar facilities and the old Roman walls. Though these Moorish walls were partially toppled by the Glorious Revolution of 1868, some sections, such as those wrapped around the Alcázar, still stand today. The Dar al-lmara, plainly put, was the core of the now-existing Royal Alcázar.

It was under the guidance of Caliph an-Nasir that a full-fledged "palatial fortress" began to materialize. Long before the layout of the Alcázar became the free-form, multifaceted arrangement that it is today, reminiscent of a medieval castle in itself from an aerial perspective, it began as a quadrangular plot of land enclosed by stone walls sealed with mud mortar. Alas, no known remnants of the Dar al-lmara or other features of the Alcázar from this period exist.

As per the disintegration of the Caliphate in 1031, Seville was converted into a "*taifa* kingdom." Al-Andalus, or the territories of Islamic Iberia, were splintered into several *taifas*, or "princely states." The Abbadid Dynasty, headed by patriarch and former *qadi* (magistrate of a Shari'a court) of Seville, Abu al-Qasim Muhammad ibn Abbad, soon surpassed, then absorbed competing Muslim caliphates, such as the Zayrids, the Hammudids, and the Amirids, amongst others, until it reigned supreme. Through al-Qasim's leadership, as well as the city's strategic proximity to the Guadalquivir and its commercial relationship with North African and

Mediterranean merchants, Seville soon dominated as the most economically, politically, and resourcefully prosperous of all the *taifas*.

The Abbadid emirs made good use of the state's tremendous wealth and continued to build upon the Alcázar, in particular expanding westward. Al-Qasim's son and heir, Emir Abbad II al-Mu'tadid, who directed much of the westward expansion, also gave the new wing its name; he called it the "Qasr al-Mubarak," otherwise known as the "Palace of Good Fortune," or the "Blessed Place" for short.

Those who ruled after Abbad II continued to improve upon the Qasr al-Mubarak with regular refurbishments and artistic additions that aligned with their faith, namely, the use of elaborate geometric patterns, from perplex figures resembling multi-pointed stars and snowflakes to overlapping shapes; elegant calligraphy etched into walls; and arabesque aesthetics, an artistic style defined by floral patterns, spirals, and a balance between symmetry and nature.

It is important to note the lack of animal and human representation in the décor of the Alcázar during this time, since doing so was against the Quran. Instead, Moorish artists focused on art born from mathematics, as this scientific field was to them a means of expression that brought them closer to Allah. The geometric art left behind by the Moorish chapter of the Alcázar is undoubtedly stunning, but it is even more extraordinary when one considers that these shapes and patterns were designed with nothing but a ruler, a pair of compasses, and the artist's rich imagination.

The sumptuous selection of handmade arabesque tiles painstakingly glued onto the lofty walls, vaulted ceilings, and floors of the Abbadid palace is another unique Moorish trait. The brilliant patterns of the wall and ceiling tiles came in swatches of lapiz-blue, greens, and other cool colors. The faded glazed tiles now seen delicately laid over the gardens and walls of the Moorish palace within the Alcázar, however, are not the original pieces. While it was the Iberian Muslims who popularized the use of "patterned walls and floor tiles," the craft was first perfected by Moorish rulers in early Persia. Given the strict rules of the "Islamic Code of Non-Representation," Muslim artists had to devise a way to enliven a room and captivate the room's owners with nothing but repetitive, yet mesmerizing abstract shapes and patterns.

To add to the mystique, exactly how the Moorish artists were able to carve the intricate swirls and floral accents that bordered the tall arches and garnished the vaulted ceilings is still a matter of dispute. Most assume that wooden scaffolding similar to the ones used by ancient Egyptian laborers was most likely used, but a few insist that such scaffolding would have never been limber enough to support the artists when confronted by tricky angles and hard-to-reach corners.

Either way, the designs and work of the Moorish artists, craftsmen, and laborers were so timelessly alluring that many of the original elements, such as the arches, tiles, and arabesque styles, were preserved, augmented, or enriched by future residents. The Moorish flavors were particularly embraced by sovereigns who ushered the Alcázar through its Gothic and Mudejar phases. A tribute to Emir Muhammad al-Mu'tamid Ibn Abbad, son of Abbad II and grandson of al-Qasim, the "Poet King of Sevilla" and the last of the Abbadid *taifa* rulers, stands in the Alcázar's *Jardin de la Galera* (Garden of the Galley) to this day.

Al-Mu'tamid was only 13 when he inherited the title of emir and the dominion of southern Spain, including Seville, in 1069. 13th century Shafi'i Islamic biographer Ibn Khallikan described the cultured king as such: "[He] was gifted with a handsome face, a body perfect in its proportions, a colossal stature, a liberal hand, penetration of intellect, presence of mind, and a just perception. By these qualities he surpassed all his contemporaries; and moreover before ambition led him to aspire after power, he had looked into literature with a close glance and an acute apprehension; so that by his quick intelligence, he acquired an abundant stock of information…With these accomplishments, [al-Mu'tamid] derived from his genius the talent of expressing his thoughts in an ornate style. He composed also pieces of verse remarkable for sweetness...expressing perfectly well what he wished to say, and displaying such excellence as caused them to be copied by literary men..."

With al-Mu'tamid in power, Seville, and in turn the Alcázar, became the principal learning center of Muslim Iberia. The emir kitted out the libraries of the Alcázar with hundreds of manuscripts in educational and fictional genres alike, and hosted routine literary meetings. He also had something of an obsession with "*majalis al-uns,*" or "carefree gatherings," attended by local wordsmiths, poets, scholars, and entertainers on a weekly basis. Regulars at these literary soirées could expect lyrical battles, live music, and endless booze.

The lute-playing Al-Mu'tamid was beloved by his subjects not only for his unparalleled way with words, but for his dedication to advancing education and protecting the rights and talents of his creative and learned subjects. Whereas Emir Abbad II was notorious for his despotism and his unsparing attitude towards his subjects, his son was a fair and liberal-minded ruler who effortlessly attracted respected writers and respectable scholars to his court in the Alcázar. His court, as Khallikan put it, was a "haling place of travelers, the rendezvous of poets, the point to which all hopes were directed and the haunt of men of talent."

As emir, Al-Mu'tamid went on to capture and claim hold of Cordoba, the kingdom of Murcia on the Costa Calida, and the Andalusian city of Jaen, among other territories. For over two decades, the emir reigned undisturbed, until King Alfonso VI of Leon and Castile raided and secured Toledo, another "chief center of Muslim scholarship," in 1085. When Al-Mu'tamid refused to shell out the tributes demanded by Alfonso, the merciless Castilian monarch dispatched his soldiers to the emir's most prized city, Seville, and laid siege to its fortress. Al-Mu'tamid stubbornly tried to hold out, but the Christian forces were far more advanced, not to mention far stronger than anticipated. It pained him to do so, but he eventually had to appeal to the sultan of the North African Almoravids, Yūsuf ibn Tāshufīn, for aid. Yūsuf, who had just recently acquired the entirety of Morocco and its military forces, quickly agreed, and in 1090, sent a legion of his "veiled warriors" to chase the Castilian and Aragonese forces out of southern Spain.

Much to the chagrin of Emir al-Mu'tamid, the resilience and opulence of the Alcázar was not lost on Yūsuf. Thus, the latter began a campaign to dethrone the former, and he eventually seized Seville and its fortress for himself. The disgraced emir was then exiled to Morocco, where he remained a prisoner in body and mind until his death.

The tribute in the Garden of the Galley is a plain, but tasteful stone column established as a way to immortalize the emir's fateful exile. Printed onto one side of the column is his name and the date of his exile – September 7, 1091 – as well as a brief passage that makes mention of his accomplishments as a poet. On the opposite side of the column are a couple of lines from one of the emir's poems, a poignant wish that was never granted to him:

"God grant that I may die in Seville,

And that our graves be opened there at the resurrection."

José Luiz Bernardes Ribeiro's picture of the Column of al-Mu'tamid

As instructed by Yūsuf and his Berber inheritors, the governmental sector of the Alcázar was temporarily suspended, for the capital of the Almoravids remained in Marrakesh. That said, Almoravid architects were ordered to further extend the palace to the banks of the Guadalquivir.

At first, the Almoravids accused the Iberian Muslims of straying from the Quran, and condemned the luxury openly exhibited by the affluent Sevillean Moors. The new government enforced rigid regulations regarding architectural styles and art forms allowed in their communities, permitting only basic shapes, rudimentary palettes, and traditional geometric patterns, which were reflected in their additions to the Alcázar. Only during the second half of their fleeting 56-year reign did the Almoravids loosen up the rules, enticed by the tempting magnificence of the Al-Andalus.

The Moorish Alcázar was most likely grander in terms of space and design than in its furnishings. Up until more recent centuries, wooden furniture was a rarity, more so in conventional Islamic societies, the main reason for this being its high cost. Timber was constantly reused, and more often set aside for the building of boats, roofs, shutters, and doors. Most of the Spanish Moors, including the royals, preferred to kneel or sit Lotus-style on plush carpets, "firmly-stuffed bolsters," and soft cushions placed atop raised platforms and projections.

The Moorish craftsmen hired by the Almoravids and other Muslim rulers of the Alcázar treated the expensive resource that was wood accordingly. Every last inch of the humble helpings apportioned to them were utilized by the scrappy artists and transformed into statement art pieces through 3 artistic techniques. First, the *mashrabiyya*, wherein "lathe-turned" wood is woven into "grilled" window screens. The second was geometric marquetry, which calls for covering surfaces with wood veneers carefully laid out side by side to create various patterns. Finally, inlay, which, as its name suggests, involves inlaying, or embedding colored chunks of wood into the crevices punched into larger tablets of wood. The one article of wooden furniture presumably owned by the Moors in Alcázar was the *minbar*, a flowery wooden throne placed atop a set of three short steps.

In early 1147, the Almoravids were ejected from their seat of power when they failed to quash an insurrection raised by Ibn Tumart. The Almoravids contended vigorously for the reins, but they were never able to recover from the bedlam incited by Tumar's revolt. Their lastflickering flame of hope was snuffed out when the Almoravid king, Ishaq ibn Ali, was assassinated in Marrakesh that April by the Almohad Caliphate.

The Almohad Caliphate once again reinstated Seville as the capital of the Al-Andalus, and the Alcázar as its governing headquarters and a place of Islamic learning. Like the previous Moroccan sovereigns, the Almohads aggrandized the metropolis with renovations and expansions to the existing Arabic architecture, concentrating especially on the grand Sevillean fortress, as well as a series of new mosques and seasonal royal residences.

The builders and designers employed by the Almohad rulers were also restricted by the society's belief in religious reformation, but this did nothing to stifle their creativity. The *Mezquita de Sevilla,* or the Grand Mosque of Seville, and the minaret-turned-bell tower, the *Torre Giralda*, are just some of the Almohad artists' magnum opuses. On top of the Almohads' penchant for geometric patterns and ornamental designs, architects and engineers integrated the rectangular arcades, splendid brick and stone facades, interlaced, as well as trademark poly-lobed arches (arches with a series of semi-circles or "lobes" for the intrados) into their plans for the Alcázar.

The Almohads, like many other Arabic rulers and sovereigns from dry nations, had a special fondness for resplendent gardens and springs, so much so that they often constructed their own springs in their palaces. Most significantly, gardens in the Quran were used as meditative spaces, and to symbolize the paradise that awaited those who subscribed to the faith. As such, several gardens were planted within and outside the walls of the Alcázar. One of these miniature vegetative paradises was a deluxe "4-part garden...with deeply sunken quadrants" known as the *"Patio de la Casa de Contratacion"* ("Courtyard of the Hiring House"). It continues to be preserved in the center of the Andalusian public works and finances offices of the modern-day Alcázar.

The courtyard was originally found within one of the buried Moorish palaces in the fortress. Like the *Patio del Crucero* (Courtyard of the Cross), the brick courtyard of the *Casa de Contratacion* was shaped like an even-armed cross, with a lush flowerbed in each quadrant, watered by 4 *acequias*, or narrow irrigation canals placed 2 meters above them. Finally, in the center of the courtyard, there was a babbling, triple-tiered fountain.

The Renaissance-era rulers of the Alcázar who later inherited the gardens elected to keep many of the plants installed by the previous tenants. Excavations during the 1970s revealed traces of centuries-old orange, lemon, and palm trees, as well as myrtle hedges, particularly in the *Huerta de la Alcoba* (Alcove Orchard). The *acequias* are thought to have been connected to the *Estanque de Mercurio* (Mercury Pool) by the Grutesco Gallery, which holds over 670 cubic meters (670,000 liters) of water.

Mihael Grmek's picture of the gardens from Galeria de Grutescos

The most well-known of all the Moorish gardens in Alcázar is the *Patio del Yeso,* or "Courtyard of Stucco"; it is also the oldest surviving segment of the original Alcázar. This *patio,* marked by its rectangular reflective pool, keyhole doors, and the webs of squid-shaped stucco tracery that crowned and filled the gaps of the poly-lobed arches, was easily the most magnificent of the courtyard within the Alcázar at the time. Bearing this in mind, the palace by the *Patio del Yeso* was reserved for the Almohad caliphs Abu Yaqub Yusuf and Abu Yusuf al-Mansur; Pedro the Cruel also lived here as he awaited the completion of his new royal residence. Christian rulers later modernized the *Patio del Yeso* by adding a *qubba,* or a "square reception hall," capped with a wooden ceiling, to the courtyard. The *qubba* remained in use for several centuries until it was retired by its occupants in the 1700s.

To the right of the Maiden's Courtyard was the *Dormitorio de los Reyes Moros*, the Bedroom of the Moorish Kings, or the *Alcoba Real*, the Royal Bedroom. The caliphs slept in this "open bedroom" to escape the sweltering summer heat. The interior was split into two chambers, accessible by an entrance composed of 3 horseshoe arches. The room to the left, the "Lost Steps Room," was outfitted with a coffered ceiling, an archway with 13 lobes, and a passageway that led straight to the patio.

A hypnotic medley of geometric tiles in all shapes and colors, paired with wooden slabs delicately inlaid with colorful tiles coated every inch of the walls and ceilings. Extravagant plaster friezes, along with patriotic medallions of Gothic-style lions were added to the walls by 15th century Catholic monarchs.

In the Alcázar the Almohad caliphs remained until Castilian King Ferdinand III reclaimed Cordoba, Mucia, and Jaen, and besieged Seville in 1247. The Almohads and Sevillean locals put up a bitter fight, hurling projectiles and tipping over buckets of boiling oil through the crenels of the Alcázar walls, and they managed to keep the Castilian invaders at bay for some time, but by the summertime, their resilience began to waver. By then, they were rapidly being picked off by famine, dehydration, and disease. They finally surrendered in November of the following year, and as stipulated by the agreement struck between the Castilian king and Almohad caliph, hundreds of thousands of Spanish Muslims were "escorted" to Granada or North Africa by Christian soldiers. Only Jews and Moriscos, or converted Muslims, were permitted to stay.

On the 22nd of December, 1248, King Ferdinand III, along with 24,000 of his subjects from Castile and Leon, marched into Seville. They were accompanied by a glittering procession, complete with a stately carriage towed by 4 white stallions and an entourage bearing the ivory statue of the "Virgin of the Kings," and beautiful maidens showering the streets with baskets of flowers. Ferdinand was the first Castilian king in 5 centuries to succeed in reclaiming Spain from the Moors.

A contemporary depiction of King Ferdinand III of Castile

Following the Reconquista, which culminated with the "Siege of Seville," Ferdinand moved his court to the Alcázar, where he remained until his death in 1252, closely followed by his canonization as Seville's patron saint. Ferdinand's son, Alfonso X, patterned his governing style after his father's, maintaining a religious tolerance that extended to his Christian, Jewish, and even Muslim subjects alike. It was this thriving, multicultural atmosphere that triggered the next stage of the fortress' development.

A contemporary depiction of Alfonso X

Gothic and Mudejar Phases

"Burn old wood, read old books, drink old wines, have old friends." – attributed to Alfonso X of Castile

Alfonso X the Wise may have shared his father's passion towards the growth of Seville, as well as his partiality for Moorish art and culture, but the palace left behind by the Muslim rulers failed to meet the king's standards of living and the requirements of the Castilian court. Whereas the Moors preferred more compact spaces with complex, labyrinthine layouts, so as to ensure the peace and solitude needed in meditation, the new occupants of the Alcázar favored proper palatial rooms in both size and grandeur. More importantly, whereas the Moors preferred a relatively uniform look throughout the entirety of their establishments, the Christian monarchs were accustomed to designing and ornamenting the different parts of the palace based on their respective "hierarchical" merits. The governmental wings, for example, would not have warranted as much attention in terms of majesty and detail when compared to the private residences of the royals.

Operating on this logic, Alfonso chose not only to expand the palace but also consciously infused into his new home Gothic elements, or as defined by the *Visual Arts Encyclopedia*, "[architectural features] which linked medieval Romanesque art with the Early Renaissance." Alfonso, like many royals of his time, was especially taken with the fresh aesthetic that aimed to blend the old with the new, a style popularized and imported from France. Furthermore, Gothic art forms were closely affiliated with the Crusaders, meaning his decision to decorate in this style was a sort of homage to Christianity's triumph over Islam. From that point forward, the once Moorish Palace was to be known as the *Palacio Gótico,* or the Gothic Palace.

Authenticity being one of Alfonso's priorities, Castilian, French, and other European architects and artists with shimmering resumes, including the very masons who assembled the immaculate interior and naves of the breathtaking Burgos Cathedral, were employed for the task. Renovations began on the 22nd of March, 1254, and the laborers' first assignment was to build a channel that would transport water from the Caños de Carmona into the Alcázar. Future sovereigns, such as Emperor Carlos V (Charles V) and King Felipe II, renovated and added their own touches to the Gothic Palace in the 16th century, but most of the original ground floor was kept as it was.

Holy Roman Emperor Charles V

The ceramic tile plinths, or "dados," that adorned the baseboards bordering the bottom halves of the palace walls, like those found in the radiant Halls of Carlos V, were designed by Cristóbal de Augusta, a potter from Navarre who was married to the daughter of a manufacturer of malioca ("tin-glazed earthenware") tiles. These plinths, often likened to tapestries, comprised two upper friezes, a lower frieze, and a central panel boxed in by its own borders, and separated by grotesques (an artistic style that combines human and animal forms with foliage). The lower strip features pairs of animals, such as lions, tigers, dragons, and mythical beasts, facing away from each other. Curly-haired cherubs, colorful birds, and serpents garnish the bottom half of the upper frieze, while the top half, on the other hand, is embellished with angels and fair maidens clutching onto the crest of the Spanish Crown, as well as columns displaying a banner with the words "Plus Ultra" ("Further Beyond)," the personal motto of Carlos V.

This sensational tile artwork is only one of the hallmarks of Carlos V's stunning hall. The place is brought to life with its Gothic vaulted ceilings and their striking wooden trimmings, and the floor-length springline windows, which bathe the walls and floors with brilliant natural light and allow those on the inside to admire the view of the gardens. Back in the day, those on the side of the palace overlooking the *Patio del Crucero* often wandered out to the upper-story walkway in the middle of the afternoon, chatting away as they snacked on sweet oranges freshly plucked from the trees within reach.

The Sala de las Bóvedas in the Gothic Palace

The Gothic Palace is also famed for the Chapel of San Clemente, installed by Alfonso in 1271. Little of the original place of worship, however, remains. The chapel is now dominated by an ornate wooden altarpiece, designed by 18th century artist Diego de Castillejo, depicting the cloaked Virgin of Antigua carrying Jesus as a child, and a white rose. Three winged angels hover over the Virgin, brandishing a bejeweled crown in their hands. Above the altarpiece itself, is a round stained glass window with the royal insignia of the Spanish Crown, wreathed by blue, violet, and yellow flowers. A rusty organ, mirror, "confessional armchair," and a medieval iron chandelier used in the chapel centuries ago can now be found on display in the Alcázar.

The only other major addition made before the reign of Pedro the Cruel in the mid-14th century was the *Sala de Justica.* Construction of this "Justice Chamber" was commissioned by King Alfonso XI, the great-grandson of Alfonso X, supposedly to commemorate his victory against the Muslims during the Battle of Salado. Builders expanded upon and revamped the *mexuar*, or public reception hall of the former Moorish palace, which was situated next to the *Patio del Yeso*. The original room had been built with the Persian *qubba*, or domed mausoleums typically used in Islamic worship; though the squareness of the space and the baroque latticework with the 8-pointed star on the ceiling were preserved, the floor tiles were replaced with warmer, reddish-brown colors. A small, circular pool rimmed with gray marble, which was hooked up to the pond in the *Patio del Yeso*, was also installed.

It was here that the Moorish Imperial Council, otherwise known as the "Council of Viziers," convened during Saracen times. When Pedro was handed the royal scepter in 1350, the *Sala de Justica* became a courtroom of sorts, where he pardoned and meted out punishments to those who he branded guilty.

Despite Pedro's alleged barbarism and the countless horror stories that continue to sully his name to this day, he was responsible for some of the most regal rooms and qualities of the Alcázar. Rarely mentioned are Pedro's surprisingly progressive foreign policies; apart from his deep admiration of Moorish and Berber culture, his cabinet was staffed with as many Moriscos as Christians, as well as plenty of Muslims and even a smattering of Jews. His unlikely alliance with the Moors bore so much weight, in fact, that he even secured a covenant of mutual assistance with more than one Nasrid Sultan from Granada so as to get a leg up on his local enemies.

Pedro's rapport with the Muslims was ultimately what allowed him to construct what many claim to be the most spectacular part of the fortress: the *Palacio del Rey Don Pedro,* or the "Palace of King Peter I." The palace, the only structure crafted from scratch – foundations included – is often referred to as the "Mudejar Palace." The term "*mudejar*," stems from the Arabic word, "*mudajian,*" or "domesticated," and denotes the "use of Islamic motifs in non-Muslim settings." In this case, the "*mudejar*" art style marries both Islamic and Christian elements, producing one beautiful fusion of a product. *Sevillano* columns (dappled marble columns crowned with gilded moldings), poly-lobed arches, thin green tiles separating blocks of voussoirs, and ornamental stucco in "sebka patterns (a network of diamond shapes)," as well as tiles, friezes, and panels with human and animal representation in Moorish art styles, are just some of the Mudejar features of the palace.

One of the gates in the Palace of Peter of Castile

Pedro's decision to depart from the Gothic art style may have also been politically motivated. While Pedro was about as Catholic as other Castilian kings, he supposedly harbored a deep resentment for the French Church, taking great offense to the Avignon popes' illegitimate children, advocacy for simony, indulgences, and other corrupt practices. He thought the Gothic art form bland, banal, and more alien than it was exotic.

Like Alfonso X, Pedro aimed for authenticity. Rather than employing random artists and laborers and instructing them to emulate Moorish aesthetics, Pedro reached out to Emir Muhammad V, one of his closest political allies, and requested from him an assemblage of the most stellar Moorish craftsmen. Most of the exceptionally talented artists, artisans, and architects who came over from Granada, Toledo, and the outskirts of Seville had personally worked on the last round of construction of the splendid Alhambra.

The Arabic and Latin inscriptions carved onto the walls and the entrance of the palace, highlighted by bright cobalt-blue tiles, are perhaps one of the best examples of cultural synthesis. "The empire of God," reads the Arabic phrase repetitiously engraved between the columns on the middle level of the palace facade. Above the three sets of poly-lobed arched windows is a blue-and-white panel with the words, "There is no conqueror but God," stamped onto it in Kufic script. Finally, the following Latin passage is etched onto the decorative strip around this panel: "The highest, noblest, and most powerful conqueror, Don Pedro, by God's grace King of Castile and Leon [sic], has caused these Alcázares and palaces and these facades to be built, which was done in the year 1364." Other epigraphs one might find in Pedro's palace include "Glory to our Lord, the Sultan Peter!," "May Allah Protect Him!," and "Only Allah is Victorious."

A picture of Arabic inscriptions glorifying the Christian rulers

Those who pieced together the *Palacio del Rey Don Pedro* plotted the structure in two parts. Half of the establishment, which houses the *Patio de las Doncellas*, or the "Damsels' Courtyard," was to be open to the public. The other half, built around the *Patio de las Muñecas,* or the "Dolls' Courtyard," was to be exclusive to the royals and other private parties.

The Patio de las Doncellas courtyard

If someone wished to access the palace, one had to pass through the *Patio de la Montería,* the "Hunting Courtyard." As hinted by its name, the courtyard was where Pedro and other royals gathered with their hunting circles before their expeditions. This was also the central *patio* of the Alcázar, and functions as the primary junction between the fortress' palaces. The courtyard was also home to a fabulous collection of remarkable flora. The walls crawled with curtains of ivy and moss. Towering cypress, palm, and fruitful banana trees sprouted from the fertile earth. Sprinkled in between them were myrtle hedges, pomegranate shrubs, floppy elephant ears that provided plenty of shade, sweeping squares of yellow, fuchsia, red, and orange lantanas, and thorny blankets of pink, red, and violet rose bougainvilleas, to name a few.

A passageway from the Hunting Courtyard, paved with colorful chessboard tiles, leads to the *Patio de las Doncellas*, also known as the "Maidens' Courtyard." This *patio,* which serves as the main courtyard of Gothic Palace, was rehabilitated, redecorated, and rechristened by Pedro sometime in the 1370s. Its name was directly inspired by a myth from antiquity in which the Christian kings of Iberia were made to pay an annual tribute of 100 virgins (half of them of noble birth) to the Islamic Emirate of Cordoba in exchange for a guarantee of their continued independence. Daniel Eisenberg, one of the authors of the *Encyclopedia of Medieval Iberia*, has denounced this as no more than an urban legend, propaganda perpetuated by Christian rulers and the 13th century Church that aimed to galvanize the Christians' ultimately successful efforts to reclaim southern Spain.

The four pools in the Maidens' Courtyard, which represent the four rivers of heaven in the Quran, as well as the four continents known to mankind during Moorish times, were among one of the major features Pedro chose to preserve. Visitors say one can best appreciate the courtyard by sitting upon a tiled recess, or alcove, in the corner of the garden. Only then can one truly marvel at the captivating arcades, the "star-patterned Mudejar *azulejos* (blue-and-white ceramic tile work often found in Spain and Portugal), " the spellbinding patterns carved into the moldings of the arches, and the fragrant cluster of orange trees in one sitting.

The courtyard provided a grand backdrop for numerous meetings, feasts, and friendly gatherings between the Christian royals and their officials; conferences were also held in the Ambassadors' Hall, the Room of the Ceiling of Felipe II, and the Room of the Half Crane, which surrounded the patio. Towards the end of the 1500s, three of the pools, as well as a few sections of the gardens were covered with marble plates and padded down with fertile soil, creating a long and narrow reflecting pool in the center of the courtyard. The gallery of white "semicircular arches," complete with matching slender columns and railing on the second floor of the open-air *patio*, was constructed during the time of King Charles I.

The Castilian kings' private courtyard, the *Patio de las Muñecas,* is visibly marked by a more personal touch. Some say it was designed specifically to suit the exquisite tastes of Pedro's queen, though it's not clear exactly which queen this was. The pretty rectangular *patio* is flanked on 4 sides by a cream-colored series of "ruffled," or poly-lobed arches and diamond-latticed haunches, shored up by short columns of white, pink, and black marble from the city of Madinat Al-Zahra.

The *patio* was given another major makeover between the years of 1847 and 1855, a project directed by esteemed woodcarver José Gutiérrez de la Vega. The floral-eqsque indentations and "cellular" carvings (*muqarnas*) on the cornices, or the molding above the arches and haunches, were added during this time. The "Neo-Mudejar" mezzanine, located between the first floor and the grilled windows on the second story, was built shortly thereafter. When the aged columns of the courtyard eventually began to show signs of cracks and crumbling, the marble specialist José Barradas was hired to replace them.

A self portrait of José Gutiérrez de la Vega

17th century historian Rodrigo Caro was among the first to ponder the etymology of the courtyard's name. The Courtyard of the Dolls, insisted Caro, was dubbed as such either because of its dainty size and character or the royal children's tendency to play with their dolls in the courtyard. Nowadays, it is believed that the courtyard was named after the minuscule chubby doll faces subtly sculpted into the curves of the courtyard's arches and pillars.

The nine smiling doll faces peppered throughout the *patio* are only a few of the Easter eggs concealed within the Alcázar. One should also be on the lookout for the golden peacocks camouflaged in the foliage swirls above the triple arch in the Ceiling Room of Philip II. Those able to discover all the Easter eggs unaided, say local mystics, are either blessed with child or good fortune.

Later Castilian kings also renamed the *Puerta de la Montería* the *"Puerta del Leon."* The *puerta,* or the "Lion's Gate" – which leads to the *Patio del Leon,* a protruding segment wedged between the *Sala de la Justica* and the *Cuarto del Almirante* (Admiral's Room) – is essentially the main entrance to the entire fortress. A black arch door was installed in the center of the crimson gate. Above the door is a tile panel – a José Gestoso original – showcasing a crowned heraldic lion with a lolling tongue, wielding a golden cross with one claw, and stomping upon what appears to be the pole of a blue flag with the other. A white sash draped around the lion, bearing the Gothic script, *"Ad Utrumque,"* or "Prepared for All," completes the picture. The

Triana tiles used in this piece were sourced from the Sevillean ceramics factory of José Mensaque y Vera.

Ian Tom Ferry's picture of the Lion's Gate

The *Los Baños de Doña María de Padilla,* a network of baths-turned-rainwater tanks underneath the *Patio del Crucero,* is yet another notable sector of the Alcázar that Pedro the Cruel had refurbished.

Even in the early years of his reign, it appeared as if Pedro had learned nothing from the marital indiscretions of his father, though in his defense, the situation was considerably more complicated. In 1353, Pedro halfheartedly exchanged his wedding vows with Blanche of Bourbon in Valladolid. This was a calculated arrangement orchestrated by Pedro's mother, Maria of Portugal, to ensure a sound relationship with the French Crown. Not only was Blanche's pedigree favorable – she was the first cousin of King John II, and the daughter of Duke Pedro I of Bourbon, the great-grandson of King Louis IX, and Isabel de Valois, the granddaughter of King Philip III – the fair-haired 14-year-old was sharp-witted, well-educated, and spiritually irrepressible.

However, unbeknownst to the queen, Pedro had already married another noblewoman – a sultry, dark-haired beauty by the name of Maria de Padilla. Though this was a fact Pedro vehemently denied, he deserted Blanche and fled to the arms of his "mistress" less than 72 hours after his marriage. Like father, like son, Pedro had a bunch of children with his paramour, a total of 14 to be exact, but only 4 would reach adulthood.

As one might expect, Pedro's impulsive divorce from Blanche incited uproar among the upper echelons of Spain and France, and on top of that, the temperamental king imprisoned his former bride. Humiliated and outraged by Pedro's actions, his mother and Aunt Leonor attempted to guilt and hector him into taking back Blanche, in no small part due to the fact they were deeply anxious about the prospect of Maria's Castilian and Portuguese relatives "stealing" the prestigious titles and privileges that belonged to them. But Pedro, the iron-willed and brutish sovereign that he was, was not to be trifled with, and anyone who dared to speak ill of the love of his life was marched to the gallows or executed in some other manner, no questions asked.

In 1361, the most radiant light in Pedro's life was extinguished when 27-year-old Maria passed away, supposedly due to a particularly ferocious outbreak of the plague. Her body was initially buried in the convent she erected, but she was later laid to rest alongside the royals in the Seville Cathedral.

Curiously, there exists another version of Pedro and Maria's love story floating around, one defiled by a dark twist. Maria, claim some chroniclers, was already a wife when Pedro first laid his eyes on her, and it was Pedro himself who arranged the murder of Maria's husband. The inconsolable and heartbroken Maria enrolled at the Santa Clara convent in a remote part of the city in a bid to find solace, but to her dismay, Pedro tracked her down. Her royal stalker was relentless, even going so far as to build a tower next to the convent for the sole purpose of spying on her. When the traumatized Maria was eventually driven to delirium by the merciless harassment, the unhinged young woman stumbled into the underground baths of the Alcázar. Once she had lured Pedro into the baths, she hoisted a barrel of boiling oil over her head and poured out its contents, willingly scalding her own face and chest. It was only then that Pedro showed some semblance of remorse, after which he finally retired his "romantic" pursuit of her and permitted her to open the Convent of Santa Inés. As darkly gripping as this tale is, only part of it is true, because while such tragic events did unfold, it happened to Maria Fernandez Coronel, most likely after the death of Maria de Padilla.

At the end of the day, of all the women in Pedro's life, it was Maria de Padilla who left the most indelible imprint. As such, to honor the memory of his one true love, Pedro renamed the part of the palace Maria frequented most after her.

Following the disastrous 9.0-magnitude earthquake that shook the neighboring city of Lisbon on the 1st of November in 1755, the Spanish government decided that another major round of renovations was in order. Half of the laborers were assigned to re-stabilizing foundations and sealing the cracks and damage sustained during the quake and ensuing aftershocks. The rest were expected to work on reorganizing, as well as adding to the compendium of dreamy gardens within the palatial complex, most notably the *Huerta de la Alcoba*, *Las Damas*, *Las Galeras*, *El Rústico*, the 18th-century *Jardin Ingles* (The English Garden), the *Jardin de los Poetas* (The Garden of the Poets), and the Grutesco Gallery, to name a few. The most noteworthy of all these gardens, past and present, is the *Jardin del Estanque*, the "Garden of the Mercury Pond." Nested in a thicket of tall, verdant trees, and fronting the Moorish loggia is a rectangular pool of twinkling water. The centerpiece of this pond is a goblet-shaped, 2-tiered fountain constructed out of volcanic stones and gritty sea gravel. Sitting atop the lower tier of the fountain is a circle of chubby cherubs with curly ringlets for hair. Below them is a circle of mythical beasts interspersed with long spouts that spurted out jets of water. Last, but not least, is the imposing bronze statue of the god Mercury depicted with his winged helmet, a gorgeous showpiece designed by 16th century Spanish sculptor Diego de Pesquera and cast by Sevillean metallurgist Bartolomé Morel.

A Timeless Work of Art

"As many languages as you know, so many separate individuals you are worth." – attributed to Holy Roman Emperor Charles V

Splendor aside, the noble tiled walls of the Alcázar have witnessed a number of momentous historical events throughout the centuries of its existence.

To begin with, the fortress has welcomed a number of royal babies over the years. Prince Juan of Asturias, for one, was born right inside the fortress walls on June 30, 1478. Queen Isabella and her husband, Ferdinand II of Aragon, may have already been the proud parents of four intelligent and courtly young women, but to them, Juan was nothing short of a miracle, for he was the only one of their sons to survive their childhoods, making him the long-awaited heir to the throne.

The royal couple made their glee no secret. For the next 3 days, the city was hectic with musical parades, thrilling dances, and lively festivities. Another round of celebrations transpired about a week after Juan's birth. That morning, a majestic procession, beginning from the Alcázar, marched through the Sevillean streets, the cavalcade concluding at the local cathedral. The star of the show was resting in the arms of his nurse, the swaddled darling slumbering comfortably in the shade provided by the brocade canopy of his carriage. Riding alongside the carriage were 8 guards, clad in black cloaks, on mule-back. Silver-cross-toting clergymen, a band of sharply dressed courtiers, a parade of drummers, and a trio of pages bearing gold blocks, silver coins, and other spangled trinkets on pillows followed suit. The oblivious but beloved toddler prince, whom Isabella lovingly referred to as her special "angel," continued to receive queues upon queues of visitors and well-wishers in the following months.

Infanta Maria Antonia, daughter of Elisabetta Farnese and King Felipe V, was also born in the Alcázar.

The Alcázar was also the perfect venue for all the theatrical pomp and pageantry that went into the weddings of the European royals. On the 10th of March, 1526, Emperor Charles V wedded his first cousin, Isabel of Portugal, under the glimmering golden cupola of the *Salon de Emajedores.* To say that their wedding was a spectacle would be an understatement. Guests enjoyed a marvelous variety show performed by acrobats, alchemists, dancers, musicians, troubadours, and masked mimes. Other activities included jousting, bull-running, and even a game of hunting. As dictated by tradition, the 50 participants gathered in the Hunting Courtyard before setting out into the nearby woods, which had been furnished with deer, boars, and bears, as per the emperor's request. One of the ponds in the fortress was also stocked with schools of fish imported from faraway lands, and they were later retrieved and utilized in various dishes for the wedding feast. The festivities lasted for over a week.

The Alcázar also hosted the wedding banquet for Infanta Elena, daughter of King Juan Carlos I and the Duchess of Lugo, and Jaime de Marichalar y Saenz de Tejada, son of the Count and Countess of Ripalda, in mid-March of 1995.

In 1987, UNESCO officially declared the Alcázar, along with the Seville Cathedral and the Archivo de Indias, a world heritage site. The statement issued by the organization succinctly encapsulates the significance and wondrous legacy of this one-of-a-kind fortress: "Together these 3 buildings form a remarkable monumental complex in the heart of Seville. The cathedral and the Alcázar – dating from the Reconquest of 1248 to the 16th century and imbued with Moorish influences – are an exceptional testimony to the civilization of the Almohads as well as that of Christian Andalusia..."

Online Resources

Other Spanish history titles by Charles River Editors

Other titles about the Alcázar of Seville on Amazon

Bibliography

Corneanu, M. (2016, October 4). Alcázar of Seville. Retrieved April 10, 2018, from https://spainattractions.es/alcazar-seville/

Editors, A. H. (2017). Royal Alcázar of Seville. Retrieved April 10, 2018, from https://en.adrianohotel.com/alcazar-of-seville

Editors, E. C. (2018). Alcazar Castle of Spain: Three of the Most Magical, Spanish-Moorish Fortresses. Retrieved April 10, 2018, from https://www.exploring-castles.com/europe/spain/alcazars/

Editors, S. S. (2012, May 6). An American in Spain, part 6: Real Alcázar of Seville. Retrieved April 10, 2018, from https://skullsinthestars.com/2012/05/06/an-american-in-spain-part-6-real-alcazar-of-seville/

Editors, F. R. (2014, October 23). The Alcázar of Seville. Retrieved April 10, 2018, from https://blog.friendlyrentals.com/en/seville/general/alcazar_seville_visit-posts-114-1_3362.htm

Editors, L. P. (2016). Real Alcázar. Retrieved April 10, 2018, from https://www.lonelyplanet.com/spain/seville/attractions/real-alcazar/a/poi-sig/411802/360736

Editors, C. C. (2017, June 21). Real Alcázar de Sevilla. Retrieved April 10, 2018, from http://www.castleholic.com/2017/06/real-alcazar-de-sevilla.html

Editors, A. S. (2013, February 11). Personalities and legends that inhabited the Alcázar in Seville return to life to become night guides. Retrieved April 10, 2018, from http://www.andalusianstories.com/the-story-of-the-day/culture/news-andalusia-seville-alcazar-night-guides/

Watson, F. F. (2014, July 5). Game of Thrones Series 5: Twelve things you didn't know about the Alcazar of Seville. Retrieved April 10, 2018, from http://scribblerinseville.com/game-of-thrones-series-5-twelve-things-you-didnt-know-about-the-alcazar-of-seville/

Watson, F. F. (2015, May 17). Game of Thrones Season 5: The Water Gardens of Dorne, aka the Alcazar of Seville. Retrieved April 10, 2018, from http://scribblerinseville.com/game-of-thrones-season-5-the-water-gardens-of-dorne-aka-the-alcazar-of-seville/

Editors, S. (2011, June 27). Primera reconstrucción virtual de un corral de comedias del s. XVII. Retrieved April 10, 2018, from http://www.agenciasinc.es/Noticias/Primera-reconstruccion-virtual-de-un-corral-de-comedias-del-s.-XVII

Valdivieso, E. (2014). The Alcazar up to the nineteenth century. Retrieved April 10, 2018, from http://www.alcazarsevilla.org/history/

Elzner, S. (2017). THE REAL ALCAZAR IN SEVILLE: PALACES OF DREAMS, GARDENS OF PLEASURE. Retrieved April 10, 2018, from http://www.happinessandthings.com/real-alcazar-seville-palace-dreams-garden-pleasure/

Steves, R. (2015). Spanish History Set in Stone. Retrieved April 10, 2018, from https://www.ricksteves.com/watch-read-listen/read/articles/spanish-history-set-in-stone

Carson, B. (2016, August 16). We visited the Spanish palace used in 'Game of Thrones' and it's even more beautiful in real life. Retrieved April 10, 2018, from http://www.businessinsider.com/visit-dorne-filming-location-in-seville-spain-2016-8#dorne-may-be-the-setting-for-one-of-the-most-despised-plotlines-in-the-game-of-thrones-tv-show-but-its-also-one-of-the-most-captivating-the-fictional-region-of-westeros-is-supposed-to-be-a-place-thats-luxurious-pleasant-and-warm-a-place-where-people-enjoyed-themselves-said-frank-doelger-executive-producer-1

Editors, M. (2014, January 12). The Most Dramatic Moment of the Middle Ages! Retrieved April 10, 2018, from http://www.medievalists.net/2014/01/the-most-dramatic-moment-of-the-middle-ages/

Belfrage, A. (2017, October 5). The spurned princess. Retrieved April 10, 2018, from https://annabelfrage.wordpress.com/tag/pedro-the-cruel/

Editors, U. H. (2017, February 15). Mistresses: María de Padilla, Practical Queen of Castile. Retrieved April 10, 2018, from http://unusualhistoricals.blogspot.tw/2017/02/mistresses-maria-de-padilla-practical.html

Rodriguez, B. (2017, Spring). Competing Images Of Pedro I: López De Ayala And The Formation Of Historical Memory. Retrieved April 10, 2018, from https://muse.jhu.edu/article/669500/pdf

Kelly, A. E. (2017, September 2). The Royal Mistress Series: Eleanor de Guzmán – The murdered mistress. Retrieved April 10, 2018, from https://www.historyofroyalwomen.com/the-royal-mistresses-series/royal-mistress-series-eleanor-de-guzman-murdered-mistress/

Belfrage, A. (2016, November 20). The king, his mistress, and his wife – A Castilian 14th century soap opera. Retrieved April 10, 2018, from https://annabelfrage.wordpress.com/tag/leonor-de-guzman/

Irving, S. (2016). Seville's Islamic Heritage. Retrieved April 10, 2018, from https://archive.islamonline.net/?p=6087

Esber, R. M. (1993, January/February). The Poet-King of Seville. Retrieved April 10, 2018, from http://archive.aramcoworld.com/issue/199301/the.poet-king.of.seville.htm

Beardsley, S. (2014, May 7). Seville: Real Alcázar sheds light on Christian, Muslim history of Spanish city. Retrieved April 10, 2018, from https://www.stripes.com/travel/seville-real-alcázar-sheds-light-on-christian-muslim-history-of-spanish-city-1.281928

Editors, S. T. (2017). The Royal Alcazar: Spain's Oldest Palace. Retrieved April 10, 2018, from http://www.seville-traveller.com/alcazar-spain/

Editors, B. V. (2017, July). Alcazar of Seville: Spain's Royal Palace. Retrieved April 10, 2018, from https://www.bellavitatravels.com/blog/2017/07/alcazar-of-seville

Editors, P. C. (2017, October 28). Real Alcazar of Seville. Retrieved April 10, 2018, from https://en.patiodelacartuja.com/blog/travel-seville/real-alcazar-of-sevilla

Editors, S. E. (2017, October 30). Step Back In Time at the Alcázar Seville, Spain. Retrieved April 10, 2018, from http://www.sapphireelmtravel.com/travel-journal/alcazar-seville-spain

Ruggles, D. F. (2012, August 23). The Alcazar of Seville & Mudejar Architectures. Retrieved April 10, 2018, from http://www.gardentaining.com/LAEP2300/virtual_tours/alcazar/alcazar pano write ups/alcazar article.pdf

Editors, S. T. (2017). Seville History. Retrieved April 10, 2018, from http://www.sevillatourist.com/history.html

Editors, T. W. (2018). Alcázar of Seville. Retrieved April 10, 2018, from https://www.thousandwonders.net/Alcázar of Seville

Editors, T. L. (2016). Fascinating Cultures and Histories of Seville. Retrieved April 10, 2018, from https://www.travelandlust.com/blog/seville-andalusia

Perez-Rodriguez, J. L. (2015, March 16). Green pigments of Roman mural paintings from Seville Alcazar. Retrieved April 11, 2018, from https://www.sciencedirect.com/science/article/pii/S0169131715001180

Editors, E. T. (2017, March 7). In the footsteps of the Moors: Seville. Retrieved April 11, 2018, from http://www.e-travelmag.com/spain/moors-seville/

Editors, W. P. (2015). The Garden of Eden, Brought to Life in the Moorish Gardens of the Alcazar of Seville. Retrieved April 11, 2018, from http://www.webphoto.ro/spain/the-garden-of-eden-brought-to-life-in-the-moorish-gardens-of-alcazar-seville.html

Editors, S. R. (2016, January 8). THE ROYAL ALCAZAR IN SEVILLE, SPAIN. Retrieved April 11, 2018, from http://simplicityrelished.com/the-royal-alcazar-in-seville-spain/

Schuermann, M. (2012, December 6). PHOTOS: Seville's Beautiful Tiles. Retrieved April 11, 2018, from https://www.huffingtonpost.com/michael-schuermann/seville-tiles-photos_b_2231468.html

Editors, V. S. (2016). Seville City. Retrieved April 11, 2018, from http://www.casanumero7.com/seville/seville.html

Editors, T. M. (2008). SEVILLE - HISTORY. Retrieved April 11, 2018, from
https://www.tripmasters.com/europe/cms/2420/Web_Content.aspx

Editors, S. C. (2016). THE ALCAZAR. Retrieved April 11, 2018, from
http://www.sevillacb.com/en/monuments/the-alcazar

Editors, D. (2017). Huerta de la Alcoba, Alcázar of Seville. Retrieved April 11, 2018, from
https://www.doaks.org/resources/middle-east-garden-traditions/catalogue/C4

Editors, D. (2017). Patio del Yeso, Alcázar of Seville. Retrieved April 11, 2018, from
https://www.doaks.org/resources/middle-east-garden-traditions/catalogue/C28

Editors, D. (2017). Patio de la Casa de Contratación, Alcázar of Seville. Retrieved April 11,
2018, from https://www.doaks.org/resources/middle-east-garden-traditions/catalogue/C9

Editors, D. (2017). Patio del Crucero, Alcázar of Seville. Retrieved April 11, 2018, from
https://www.doaks.org/resources/middle-east-garden-traditions/catalogue/C10

Editors, C. C. (2017, August 10). Los 12 personajes del Alcazar de Sevilla. Retrieved April 11,
2018, from https://conocemiciudad.com/12-personajes-alcazar-sevilla/

Editors, S. O. (2014). The Royal Alcazar palace - Seville. Retrieved April 11, 2018, from
http://www.sevillaonline.es/english/seville/alcazar-palace.htm

Curtius, Q. (2018, March 21). Reversal Of Fortune: The Fate Of Al-Mu'tamid Ibn Abbad,
Ruler Of Seville. Retrieved April 11, 2018, from https://qcurtius.com/2018/03/21/reversal-of-
fortune-the-fate-of-al-mutamid-ibn-abbad-ruler-of-seville/

Editors, E. B. (2014, December 18). Al-Mu'tamid. Retrieved April 11, 2018, from
https://www.britannica.com/biography/al-Mutamid-Abbadid-ruler-1027-1095

Editors, T. O. (2009, March 15). Water in Islamic Architecture. Retrieved April 11, 2018, from
http://throughtheoculus.blogspot.tw/2009/03/water-in-islamic-architecture.html

Editors, M. M. (2016). Http://micamara.es/real-alcazar-de-sevilla/. Retrieved April 11, 2018,
from http://micamara.es/real-alcazar-de-sevilla/

Editors, W. M. (2010, October 20). A Brief History of Seville, Spain. Retrieved April 11,
2018, from http://www.worldmonumentphotos.com/blog.php?articleID=7

Metts, S. (2016, May 31). Fernando III of Castilla: Saint, King, and Conqueror. Retrieved
April 11, 2018, from https://catholicexchange.com/fernando-iii-of-castilla-saint-king-conqueror

Editors, N. (2011, April 14). St. Ferdinand III of Castile and Leon extends the Reconquista to Seville and the south of Spain. Retrieved April 11, 2018, from http://www.nobility.org/2011/04/14/st-ferdinand-iii-of-castile-and-leon-extends-the-reconquista-to-seville-and-the-south-of-spain/

Editors, J. N. (2017, May 13). It's the real deal! Visiting Real Alcazar, Seville. Retrieved April 11, 2018, from http://journeyofanomadicfamily.com/real-alcazar-seville/

Editors, E. B. (2018, January 12). Order of Santiago. Retrieved April 11, 2018, from https://www.britannica.com/topic/Order-of-Santiago

Smith, W., LLD. (2017). Collegium. Retrieved April 11, 2018, from http://penelope.uchicago.edu/Thayer/E/Roman/Texts/secondary/SMIGRA*/Collegium.html

Gould, A. (2013, May 27). The Ancient Churches of Spain. Retrieved April 11, 2018, from https://www.orthodoxartsjournal.org/the-ancient-churches-of-spain/

Editors, C. N. (2018, April 4). ST. ISIDORE OF SEVILLE. Retrieved April 11, 2018, from https://www.catholicnewsagency.com/saint/st-isidore-of-seville-425

Editors, A. (2013). Seville City - City Walls and Gates. Retrieved April 11, 2018, from http://www.andalucia.com/cities/seville/muralla.htm

Bellos, A. (2015, February 10). Muslim rule and compass: The magic of Islamic geometric design. Retrieved April 11, 2018, from https://www.theguardian.com/science/alexs-adventures-in-numberland/2015/feb/10/muslim-rule-and-compass-the-magic-of-islamic-geometric-design

Williamson, A. (2017). The Art of Arabesque. Retrieved April 11, 2018, from http://artofislamicpattern.com/resources/introduction-to-islimi/

Reach, Z. (2017, February 13). THE SCAFFOLDING JOURNAL – THE HISTORY OF SCAFFOLDS. Retrieved April 11, 2018, from http://blog.oasismetal.net.ae/scaffolding-journal-history-scaffolds/

Editors, P. W. (2015, November 14). The Poet-King of Seville. Retrieved April 12, 2018, from https://postcardwritings.wordpress.com/2015/11/14/the-poet-king-of-seville/

Editors, A. A. (2015, August 5). Arab Spain's Poet King. Retrieved April 12, 2018, from http://www.arabamerica.com/arab-spains-poet-king/

Editors, E. B. (2014, April 17). Almoravids. Retrieved April 12, 2018, from https://www.britannica.com/topic/Almoravids

Editors, A. (2015). ALMORAVIDS AND ALMOHADS: 11TH TO 13TH CENTURIES. Retrieved April 12, 2018, from http://www.andalucia.com/spainsmoorishhistory/almoravidsandalmohads.htm

Editors, T. M. (2001, October). The Art of the Almoravid and Almohad Periods (ca. 1062–1269). Retrieved April 12, 2018, from https://www.metmuseum.org/toah/hd/almo/hd_almo.htm

Bloom, J. M. (2012, January 2). The Masterpiece Minbar. Retrieved April 12, 2018, from http://islamic-arts.org/2012/the-masterpiece-minbar/

Editors, D. I. (2015). The Muslim West. Retrieved April 12, 2018, from http://www.discoverislamicart.org/gai/ISL/page.php?theme=4

Editors, A. N. (2011). Mezquita de Sevilla. Retrieved April 12, 2018, from https://archnet.org/sites/2753/media_contents/2124

Garcia, M. (2013, April 3). Patio de la casa de contratación de Sevilla. Retrieved April 12, 2018, from http://www.paisajistasmarbella.com/2013/04/patio-de-la-casa-de-contratacion-de-sevilla/

Editors, D. (2018). What is the Royal Alcazar of Seville? Retrieved April 12, 2018, from https://www.dosde.com/discover/en/the-royal-alcazar-of-seville/

Editors, E. W. (2017, March 12). Palacio Gótico. Retrieved April 12, 2018, from https://es.wikipedia.org/wiki/Real_Alcázar_de_Sevilla#Palacio_Gótico

Cárdenas, M. (2014). Palacio Gótico del Alcázar de Sevilla. Retrieved April 12, 2018, from https://serturista.com/espana/palacio-gotico-del-alcazar-de-sevilla/

Tatford, P. (2015, December 21). Seville - The Alcázar Royal Palace. Retrieved April 12, 2018, from https://www.spain-holiday.com/Seville-city/articles/seville-the-alcazar-royal-palace

Sullivan, M. A. (2005). El Alcázar--page 2 (of nine pages): Exterior facade, Palacio del Rey Don Pedro (King Don Pedro's Palace). Retrieved April 12, 2018, from https://www.bluffton.edu/homepages/facstaff/sullivanm/spain/seville/alcazar/alcazar2.html

Editors, E. W. (2016, December 28). Patio de la Montería. Retrieved April 12, 2018, from https://es.wikipedia.org/wiki/Patio_de_la_Montería

Watson, F. F. (2016, February 17). Seville's Most Beautiful Palace. Retrieved April 12, 2018, from http://www.thespainscoop.com/the-alcazar-real-of-seville/

Editors, D. I. (2016). Seville Citadel. Retrieved April 12, 2018, from http://www.discoverislamicart.org/database_item.php?id=monument;ISL;es;Mon01;26;en

Lorente, V. L. (2014, June). Reales Alcázares de Sevilla. Retrieved April 12, 2018, from http://www.arteguias.com/alcazar/realesalcazaressevilla.htm

Editors, E. W. (2018, February 8). Patio del León. Retrieved April 12, 2018, from https://es.wikipedia.org/wiki/Patio_del_León

Editors, E. W. (2018, January 2). Puerta del León (Real Alcázar de Sevilla). Retrieved April 12, 2018, from https://es.wikipedia.org/wiki/Puerta_del_León_(Real_Alcázar_de_Sevilla)

Editors, F. P. (2017, November 13). Peter of Castile Biography. Retrieved April 12, 2018, from https://www.thefamouspeople.com/profiles/peter-of-castile-6886.php

Editors, S. D. (2009, September 3). Alcázar (3): La Sala de la Justicia. Retrieved April 13, 2018, from http://sevilladailyphoto.blogspot.tw/2009/09/el-mes-del-alcazar-3-la-sala-de-la.html

Editors, T. S. (2003, October). Royal Palace in Sevilla - The Courtyard of the Maidens. Retrieved April 13, 2018, from http://www.travelinginspain.com/sevilla/Doncellas.htm

Editors, E. W. (2018, January 23). María de Padilla. Retrieved April 13, 2018, from https://es.wikipedia.org/wiki/María_de_Padilla

Editors, S. P. (2014, November 10). Baños de María de Padilla (Sevilla). Retrieved April 13, 2018, from https://sevillapedia.wikanda.es/wiki/Baños_de_María_de_Padilla_(Sevilla)

Editors, T. B. (2011, September 27). Baños de María Padilla. Real Alcázar de Sevilla. Retrieved April 13, 2018, from http://tectonicablog.com/?p=37919

Editors, R. S. (2012, January 16). El Baño de María Padilla. Retrieved April 13, 2018, from http://descubriendosevilla2012.blogspot.tw/2012/01/el-bano-de-maria-padilla.html

Editors, E. (2011). Fadrique Alfonso of Castile. Retrieved April 13, 2018, from http://enacademic.com/dic.nsf/enwiki/1309724

Editors, V. A. (2008). Gothic Art (c.1150-1375). Retrieved April 13, 2018, from http://www.visual-arts-cork.com/history-of-art/gothic.htm

Editors, O. R. (2014). Cristóbal de Augusta. Retrieved April 13, 2018, from http://www.oxfordreference.com/view/10.1093/oi/authority.20110803095434213

Editors, A. T. (2018). MAIOLICA GRIGIO. Retrieved April 13, 2018, from https://www.artistictile.com/maiolica-grigio-cmaigrg8

Sullivan, M. A. (2005). El Alcázar--page 9 (of nine pages): Palacio Gótico (also known as the Halls of Charles V). Retrieved April 13, 2018, from https://www.bluffton.edu/homepages/facstaff/sullivanm/spain/seville/alcazar/alcazar9.html

Nelson, L. H. (2013). The Avignon Papacy, 1305-1378. Retrieved April 13, 2018, from http://www.vlib.us/medieval/lectures/avignon.html

Eisenberg, D. (2016). Slavery. Retrieved April 13, 2018, from http://users.ipfw.edu/jehle/deisenbe/Enc_of_Medieval_Iberia/Slavery.pdf

Editors, E. W. (2017, November 11). María Fernández Coronel. Retrieved April 13, 2018, from https://es.wikipedia.org/wiki/María_Fernández_Coronel

Editors, S. (2018). Joaquin Sorolla y Bastida. Retrieved April 13, 2018, from http://www.sothebys.com/en/auctions/ecatalogue/lot.60.html/2013/19th-century-european-art-n08989

Editors, I. S. (2018). Royal Alcazar of Seville. Retrieved April 13, 2018, from https://www.inspain.org/en/extraSites/royalalcazarofsevilleartisticintroduction.asp

Editors, I. S. (2018). Historical Introduction. Retrieved April 13, 2018, from https://www.inspain.org/en/extraSites/royalalcazarofsevillehistoricalintroduction.asp

Editors, M. P. (2017). LOS TAPICES DEL ALCAZAR DE SEVILLA. Retrieved April 13, 2018, from https://marcopolito56.wordpress.com/pueblos-con-encanto/los-tapices-del-alcazar-de-sevilla/

Editors, T. F. (2017). The Conquest of Tunis series. Retrieved April 13, 2018, from http://tapestries.flandesenhispania.org/index.php/The_Conquest_of_Tunis_series

Cavendish, R. (2003, January). The Casa de Contratacion Established in Seville. Retrieved April 13, 2018, from https://www.historytoday.com/richard-cavendish/casa-de-contratacion-established-seville

Editors, E. B. (2007, March 22). Casa de Contratación. Retrieved April 13, 2018, from https://www.britannica.com/topic/Casa-de-Contratacion

Gutierrez, S. (2017, February 14). El Alcázar de Sevilla, un Palacio Real de ensueño. Retrieved April 13, 2018, from http://www.elpasodelhombre.com/el-alcazar-de-sevilla-un-palacio-real-de-ensueno/

Editors, L. S. (2014, May 30). Reales Alcázares de Sevilla, -IV. Antigua Casa de la Contratación, Cuarto del Almirante, Sala de Audiencias y Sala de los Abanicos. Retrieved April

13, 2018, from http://leyendasdesevilla.blogspot.tw/2014/05/reales-alcazares-de-sevilla-iv-antigua.html

Martin, J. X. (2017). The Columbus Crocodile. Retrieved April 13, 2018, from http://jxmartin.com/Joseph_X._Martin/Columbus_Crocodile.html

Minster, C. (2017, September 2). The Second Voyage of Christopher Columbus. Retrieved April 13, 2018, from https://www.thoughtco.com/the-second-voyage-of-christopher-columbus-2136700

Sullivan, M. A. (2005). El Alcázar--page 3 (of nine pages): Chapel of the Casa de la Contratación and other details. Retrieved April 13, 2018, from https://www.bluffton.edu/homepages/facstaff/sullivanm/spain/seville/alcazar/alcazar3.html

Editors, G. T. (2018). Alcázar of Seville. Retrieved April 13, 2018, from http://www.gameofthronesspain.com/film-location/alcazar-of-seville.php

Szalay, J. (2017, September 20). Amerigo Vespucci: Facts, Biography & Naming of America. Retrieved April 13, 2018, from https://www.livescience.com/42510-amerigo-vespucci.html

Navarro, J. A. (2009, December 12). Hall of Ambassadors, Alcazar of Sevilla. Retrieved April 13, 2018, from https://www.360cities.net/image/hall-of-ambassadors-sevilla

Editors, F. H. (2015, April 10). Juan, Prince of Asturias. Retrieved April 13, 2018, from https://thefreelancehistorywriter.com/2015/04/10/juan-prince-of-asturias/

Editors, U. M. (2017). Real Alcázar. Retrieved April 13, 2018, from http://unesco.urbanismosevilla.org/unesco/en/heritage/humanidad/real-alcázar

Casas, C. (2015, May 21). The Birth of Philip II of Spain. Retrieved April 13, 2018, from https://tudorsandotherhistories.wordpress.com/category/isabella-of-portugal/

Editors, B. N. (2006). Royal Wedding in a Palace. Retrieved April 13, 2018, from http://babelnet.sbg.ac.at/themepark/castle/wedding_page.htm

Editors, U. (2018). Cathedral, Alcázar and Archivo de Indias in Seville. Retrieved April 13, 2018, from https://whc.unesco.org/en/list/383

Maugham, W. S. (2015). *The Land of The Blessed Virgin: Sketches and Impressions in Andalusia*. Simon & Schuster.

Ruiz, A. (2007). *Vibrant Andalusia: The Spice of Life in Southern Spain*. Algora Publishing.

Villalon, A., & Kagay, D. (2017). *To Win and Lose a Medieval Battle: Nájera (April 3, 1367), A Pyrrhic Victory for the Black Prince*. BRILL.

Free Books by Charles River Editors

We have brand new titles available for free most days of the week. To see which of our titles are currently free, click on this link.

Discounted Books by Charles River Editors

We have titles at a discount price of just 99 cents everyday. To see which of our titles are currently 99 cents, click on this link.

CPSIA information can be obtained
at www.ICGtesting.com
Printed in the USA
BVHW050209020323
659550BV00013B/327